Illegal Entry

by Clem Martini

Playwrights Canada Press
Toronto • Canada

Illegal Entry © Copyright 1994 Clem Martini
Playwrights Canada Press
54 Wolseley St., 2nd fl. Toronto, Ontario CANADA M5T 1A5
Tel: (416) 703-0201 Fax: (416) 703-0059
e-mail: cdplays@interlog.com   http://www.puc.ca

We acknowledge the support of The Canada Council for the
Arts for our publishing programme, and the Ontario Arts
Council.

*Cover photo: Stephen Spender (floor), Matt Embry (front),
Matthew Woodward (back), Alberta Theatre Projects, Calgary,
1995.*
Photo by Trudi Lee. Playwright photo by Donald Denton.

Canadian Cataloguing in Publication Data
Martini, Clem, 1956 —
    Illegal entry
A play
ISBN 0-88754-569-6
I. Title.
PS8576.A7935I44 1999   C812.54   C99-931061-5
PR9199.3.M3877I44 1999

First edition: November, 1999.
Printed and bound by Hignell Printing, Winnipeg, Canada.

To Cheryl, Chandra, and Miranda who have been my greatest supporters and tireless advocates all the way down the line,

and the kids at Woods Homes who have continued to surprise and inspire me in all my work with them.

An award-winning playwright, screenwriter, and writer of short fiction, Clem Martini is best known for his plays which have received productions in theatres across the country. "Selling Mr. Rushdie", "The Life History of the African Elephant", "Conversations with My Pitbull", "Up On The Roof", "Nobody of Consequence", "Bite Me & Borrow Me", and "Turnaround" are only some of his more-recently produced works. When not at his computer writing, Mr. Martini can be found teaching at the University of Calgary or working with troubled young people through the charitable organisation, Woods Home.

Playwright's Foreword

   Illegal Entry was conceived in reaction to a portrayal of troubled teens I've been accustomed to seeing in film, television, and the theatre. This paradigm portrays at-risk youth as tough, sexy, savvy, terse, and dangerous — kind of like younger, poorer versions of the international spies one sees in movies. The trouble is, this paradigm doesn't remotely resemble the guys I've worked with over the past decade who, it seems to me, most often are hurt, hopelessly screwed-over, inarticulate, and trying like mad to make sense of and cope with life. Garland, Stuart, and Jim are neither masterminds nor monsters. Unfortunately this doesn't make them any less dangerous to the public or to themselves.

PRODUCTION HISTORY

"Illegal Entry" was first produced by Alberta Theatre Projects, Calgary, as part of <u>playRites '95</u>, with the following cast:

STUART	*Matthew Woodward*
GARLAND	*Stephen Spender*
JIM	*Matt Embry*

Directed by Daniel Libman.
Set design by John Dinning.
Costume design by Carolyn Smith.
Lighting design by Brian Pincott.
Composer - Allan Rae.
Production dramaturge - Eugene Stickland.
Stage Manager - Diane Goodman.
Assistant to the designers - Colin Ross.

"Illegal Entry" was subsequently produced in the 1996/97 season of 25th Street Theatre, Saskatoon, Saskatchewan, with the following cast:

STUART	*Jacques Poulin-Denis*
GARLAND	*Christopher Lee Fassbender*
JIM	*Rodrigo Pino Hellman*

Directed by Tom Bentley Fisher.
Costume, lighting, set design by Colin Ross.
Stage Manager - Kathy Allen.
Fight director - Kent Allen.

CAST

GARLAND   A tough-looking, tough-talking, seventeen
                year old kid. Stocky in build.

JIM   Sixteen years old and tall for his age.

STUART   The youngest of the three. Fifteen. Quiet
                and very reserved.

RUNNING TIME: 75 minutes.

PRODUCTION NOTES:

The fire called for at the end of the play may be shown on
stage, as it was in the first production or, if there is no budget
for pyrotechnics, it may be desirable for Jim to fall behind the
equipment at the back of the garage when the fire erupts.

Act One

The exterior of a garage from the back alley. Late at night. The only light coming from the moon and the street lights further up the block at the end of the alley. Two teens enter and look about — STUART and GARLAND.

GARLAND   Jim?

They both look about.

GARLAND   Jim?

They peer about some more.

STUART   This is it?

GARLAND   Yea. What's the time?

STUART   One.

GARLAND   Where is he?

GARLAND peers down the side of the garage.

GARLAND   He wouldn't'a gone in already, would he?

GARLAND knocks lightly on the garage door.

GARLAND   Jim? Jim?

No answer.

GARLAND   Shit.

STUART   Listen.

GARLAND   What?

          They listen. An owl sounds in the distance.

STUART   An owl.

GARLAND   What the fuck do I care it's an owl. Jesus, don't do that. I think you're talking about Jim or the cops, I don't know what. Owls, owls, I mean what are owls? Pigeons with night vision, fuck 'em. Owls. Look, you see Jim anywhere?

STUART   No.

GARLAND   Well, let's go. We'll check back in five minutes, maybe he'll be here then. Come on.

          An owl hoots. STUART stops to listen.

STUART   There it is again.

GARLAND   Will you stop with the freakin' owls.

          GARLAND grabs STUART. They head down the block. Moments later JIM enters. He stops in front of the garage door. He looks about.

JIM   Garland?

          He now peers about.

JIM   Garland?

          He looks up each side of the garage. He hears something in the alley.

JIM   Garland, that you?

          A dog barks.

JIM   Shhh. Shhh. Will ya fuckin' shhh. Come on, shhh. Here.

He reaches into the garbage can next to the garage and pulls out some old bone.

JIM   Here's something to chew on.

The dog stops barking. JIM looks around some more.

JIM   Garland?

No answer.

Screw it. I'm going in.

He rethinks.

No, I better wait.

He waits a brief moment.

That's long enough.

Out of his jacket he pulls a remote control garage opener. He points it at the garage and presses the button. Nothing happens.

JIM   What's going on?

He presses the button again.

Shit.

Presses the button again. Looks around.

Where is he? What are you supposed to point this thing at?

He points the remote at the four corners of the garage and presses the button. Nothing.

JIM   Sonofabitch.

He tucks the remote away.

JIM   Where is he? I gotta pee.

He peers up and down the alley, and then decides to relieve himself against the corner of the garage. He unzips — no one coming. He takes out his penis — no one coming. He's about to pee, when suddenly the dog starts barking again.

JIM zips up his pants.

JIM   Shit. Sh. Quiet ... Sh, sh, sh. Quiet doggee, quiet, quiet ... look, here's another piece of meat or something from the garbage here. Eat that.

The dog chews the gristle thrown to it.

JIM   You like that? Is that good? Yummy? I hope you choke on it.

JIM once again looks up and down the alley. He goes to the corner of the garage, looks up and down. Pulls his zipper down. He is just beginning to pee, when GARLAND and STUART reappear.

GARLAND   What're you doing?

JIM   Shit.

JIM re-zips but manages to get himself caught in the zipper.

JIM   Ah! Sonofabitch! Ow! Ow! Ow!

GARLAND   Sh!

JIM   (*quieter than before*) Ow! Ow! Ow!

GARLAND   What are you doing?

JIM	I had to go.
GARLAND	Why here? Why not down the alley?
JIM	Here or down the alley, what's the difference?
GARLAND	You don't want to attract attention—
JIM	It was a quiet pee, alright? I didn't sing at the same time—
GARLAND	—and the police can use that stuff if they investigate.
JIM	Fuck off.
GARLAND	Yea.
JIM	They can't use pee.
GARLAND	Sure they can.
JIM	That's bullshit.
GARLAND	Look, if they can use blood and semen, you think they can't use *piss?*
JIM	It'll dry up in a moment and then—
GARLAND	Think about it. Dogs use piss to mark territory, one dog can tell, by piss alone, if another dog has come by five minutes or five days ago. That's *dogs.* Human piss is a hundred times more evolved than that.
JIM	*Okay.*
	Pause.
GARLAND	Now wipe it off.
JIM	*What?*

GARLAND	Wipe it off!
JIM	You're fulla shit.
GARLAND	I'm telling you—
JIM	With what? You think I'm carrying around a rag or something—
GARLAND	With grass or whatever.
JIM	Aw for—
GARLAND	Go on.

JIM picks up a handful of grass and scours the garage.

JIM	There. Happy?
GARLAND	Great. Now, let's go in.

JIM reaches into his pocket and sees STUART.

JIM	What's he doin' here?
GARLAND	I brought him along.
JIM	We didn't talk about him.
GARLAND	He knows his way 'round.
JIM	So?
GARLAND	So he's good at this.
STUART	I broke into a lotta places before.
JIM	The deal was just the two of us and we don't need someone to break in.

He holds up garage opener.

JIM	We can just walk in.

GARLAND	It's done. He's here. Let's go.
JIM	Why didn't you say something?
GARLAND	I didn't have a chance, let's *go*, before someone sees us.

Pause.

JIM	So, what do you point it at?
GARLAND	What do you mean?
JIM	Do you point it at a certain spot?
GARLAND	You point it at the door.
JIM	I already tried that. It doesn't work.
GARLAND	Just push the button.
JIM	I did.

He pushes the button.

See?

GARLAND	Let me have it.

GARLAND takes it and pushes the button.

Did you knock it or anything?

JIM	No.
GARLAND	You're sure this was working—
JIM	It was working! Just three weeks ago the guy dropped it on his way outta here with his car, left it behind, I picked it up.
GARLAND	I wonder, maybe they changed the frequency—

> *JIM snatches it back, pushes the button several
> times and flings it down.*

JIM   Shit! No!

GARLAND   Maybe they figured something like this
             might happen-

> *STUART looks down at the remote control
> and delicately steps on the button with his
> foot.*

STUART   The light's not flashing.

GARLAND   What?

STUART   The light. In the corner. It's supposed to
             flash when you push it.

GARLAND   Is that right?

JIM   It used to. Doesn't it anymore?

> *GARLAND picks it up and pushes the button.*

GARLAND   No.

JIM   Lemme see it.

> *GARLAND hands it to him.*

JIM   It's not.

> *He shakes it.*

STUART   Battery could be dead.

JIM   It was lighting up, just...

> *He shakes it.*

             ... a few ... days back—

GARLAND   You kept playing with it—

JIM   I wasn't playing with it!

GARLAND   I *told* you—

JIM   I was *testing* it!

GARLAND   How can you *test* it, without a frigging *door?*
            "Just put it away until we're ready to use it",
            I said—

JIM   Maybe it's just ... loose...

GARLAND   You tell us you have this great deal, this
            place we can just walk into. We all go
            AWOL—

JIM   I didn't invite *him*—

GARLAND   — and then you fuck away the battery.

JIM   We can get more batteries.

GARLAND   With what money, genius?

JIM   We rip off a store.

GARLAND   What store? What store is open right now, or
            are you suggesting we go back to the cottage,
            hang out 'til a store is open and then go
            AWOL again at a more appropriate time?

JIM   Shit! I don't know.

            The dog starts barking.

GARLAND   Great.

JIM   Sh, dog. Sh. There's another bone here.
            That's a fella.

GARLAND   Here. You take a look at it.

            *GARLAND offers it to STUART. STUART
            takes a step back.*

STUART   No.

GARLAND   What's the matter?

STUART   There's dew, or something on it.

GARLAND   Oh.

                GARLAND wipes it off on his sleeve.

                There.

                *STUART leans over and peers at it, then
                gingerly takes it. He opens up the back, repacks
                the batteries, and closes it back up. The dog
                quiets. STUART presses the button. The
                garage door starts to glide open.*

GARLAND   What did you do?

STUART   I repacked the batteries. Sometimes you get a
                little more out of them that way.

JIM   Yes!

GARLAND   All right.

JIM   Excellent.

                *The garage door stands open for them. A light
                wind passes by and something rattles softly
                within.*

JIM   I knew this mother would get us in. I knew it.
                Now all we have to do is walk in, just walk
                in, and take what we want like, like a, super
                market. You thought the batteries were
                finished, but I knew. Didn't I tell you?

GARLAND   Great, it's just like a super market. So, let's
                walk in.

                They walk in.

STUART   I hope there's candy.

JIM   Candy?

STUART   I like candy.

GARLAND   Okay. Shut the door. Or you want the whole world to see us breaking into the freaking house?

JIM pushes the button. Nothing. He points it up, and pushes. Nothing.

JIM   It won't shut.

GARLAND   Aw Christ, give it here—

JIM   Gimme a minute.

The garage door light which had gone on when the door opened, begins to fade.

JIM   Hey, what's that?

GARLAND   The lights are on a timing mechanism. Will you come on! Wave to the folks across the alley, Stuart.

JIM   What'd you do to it again?

But at that moment the mechanism kicks in. The garage door begins closing.

JIM   There!

GARLAND   Okay.

JIM   Easiest B&E ever.

GARLAND   Great.

We see the last of their feet, then the stage revolves and we see the three teens in the garage, in the dark.

GARLAND   Terrific.

     GARLAND turns on his flashlight.

GARLAND   So, let's go.

     They walk to the back door and STUART looks at it.

STUART   Can you shine the light up a bit closer?

     GARLAND finds the overhead light switch and flicks it. They have light.

GARLAND   There we go. Should be okay with this.

     STUART examines the door. Tries to pull it open, then taps on it.

STUART   Oh oh.

GARLAND   What?

     Pause while STUART taps some more on various parts of the door.

JIM   What?

STUART   We're not going through this door.

GARLAND   What's wrong?

     STUART raps on the door again.

STUART   It's metal. And there are two dead bolts.

GARLAND   You're kidding? Who puts that kinda door in a garage?

JIM   What about the hinges?

STUART   They're on the other side. We'd have to cut through it with a blow torch.

GARLAND   Son of a bitch. Who puts a metal door with
          two dead bolts between their garage and
          their own house? The guy who owns this
          place must be a freaking paranoid.

JIM   Maybe the keys are in here.

          GARLAND looks at him.

          Y'know, like hung on the wall somewhere.

GARLAND   Right. Like the guy who puts this kinda door
          in is going to just hang his keys up, God
          you're a dimbulb sometimes.

          GARLAND taps on the door.

          Son of a bitch. I don't know. Let's see what
          we got here. Sleeping bags, pop cans, tent,
          bikes — this isn't a garage, it's a rummage
          sale waiting to happen — paint and paint
          thinner, a vice, electric sander. Electric
          sander? This is good.

          *On the work table, next to a vice, lies an
          electric sander. GARLAND picks up the
          sander.*

          Where there's an electric sander, there're
          other tools. We find a blade and we can cut
          our way round the lock. Take a look.

          The guys search the garage.

STUART   Old rags. Coupl'a back packs. More paint and
          thinner. A window pane. Nothing.

JIM   Keys!

GARLAND   Keys?

JIM   Ya, right here, on the workbench, *wanker.*

GARLAND   Ya, ya. Throw 'em here.

JIM tosses the keys to garland.

GARLAND   As if these are door keys, ya limpwick.

JIM   Well, what are they keys for then?

GARLAND   Duh, maybe the cabinet here above the workbench, you think? Maybe we got tools here.

GARLAND unlocks the cabinet.

Right on. Tools!

GARLAND starts unloading the cabinet.

Extension cord. A radio! Tunes! And ... *another electric sander?* The guy's a sanding nut! And that's it.

He takes a thorough look at the cabinet.

There any other cabinets?

STUART   Nope.

GARLAND   What kind of guy has two electric sanders in his garage, and no other appliance? I mean, what can he be sanding? (*finding sand paper*) Oh yea, and extra sand paper. Great. What are you doing over there dip shit?

JIM   Looking at the paint and thinner.

GARLAND   We already know there's paint and thinner, will ya look for something else?

JIM   We could use the thinner.

GARLAND   How?

JIM   We could pour the thinner on the door and torch it.

GARLAND   It's metal.

JIM   We could pour the thinner around the door, torch it, and the door'll fall in.

GARLAND   Whew. (*shaking his head*) Sometimes you amaze me. You torch the door, you know what's going to happen? Every fire alarm in that house is going to go off, and you know what else is going to happen?

JIM   What?

GARLAND   This garage is going to go up like a rocket. What are you going to put this fire out with, Smokey? Douse it with house paint?

JIM   Just put a little on. What else are we going to do? Turn around and leave?

            Pause.

            No way. No way, we can't just leave? We just got here.

GARLAND   What else can we do? We can't get it.

JIM   There's stuff in that house to be *had*, man. We didn't go AWOL together just to turn round and go back. What about our trip?

GARLAND   We got a bike, two sanders and a radio. Beer money. We can party. Let's go.

JIM   You're not serious?

GARLAND   We *can't get in*.

JIM   We just got here.

GARLAND   We *can't get in!*

STUART   Jim—

JIM   Shut up! I didn't come up here just to walk away empty handed!

GARLAND   How many times we gotta say it, we can't get in! The whole thing was you found the garage opener and we could slip in, grab some stuff easy, and go, but we can't, so let's go before someone calls the cops.

JIM   We could break a window in the house.

GARLAND   Right. And we could phone the cops ourselves. Look, the whole thing is not to be caught, right? Right? So, we don't want to be smashing windows and climbing in for the world to see like a bunch'a eight year olds. It was a good idea you had, it didn't work, it's nobody's fault, it happens. That's all.

      Pause.

      Jim? Come on.

JIM   Sonofabitch.

      Pause.

      Sonofabitch, this fucking door!

      JIM throws himself against the door.

      Open up, you sonofabitch. Open up!

      JIM tosses a box of cans against the door.

GARLAND   What are you doing? Will you chill?

STUART   Cut it out. Jim!

      JIM throws another box of cans.

GARLAND   Grab him!

      They wrestle.

JIM   Let go of me!

GARLAND   The cops'll be here for sure if you don't settle.

JIM   I *said* let go!

JIM breaks free and grabs the pane of glass resting against the wall. He spins about and hurls it across the garage.

GARLAND   Don't.

JIM   *SHIT!*

The glass shatters with an enormous crash. The three stand, stunned.

GARLAND   You are the stupidest piece of business I have ever worked with—

JIM   Shut up.

GARLAND   No, *you* shut up. The idea is to get in and out *quietly* and without leaving any sign that we've been here except that we took something and you go shatter a freaking window against the wall. Why not set off fireworks, asshole? The Help will be here any time now, let's go. Gimme that.

GARLAND snatches the garage opener and presses the button. Nothing happens.

GARLAND   It's outta juice now. Hit the switch on the wall, next to the light switch.

STUART flicks the switch. Nothing happens.

STUART   It's not working.

GARLAND   (*to himself*) Now what? (*investigating the switch*) Is this the thing? Yea, this should open the door.

> *GARLAND flicks it several times but ...*
> *nothing.*

GARLAND   What's going on? (*looking up at the ceiling*)
           Shit.

STUART   What?

GARLAND   There's the problem. Your glass smashed the
           thingy up there at the top, asshole. (*moving
           to the garage door*) Where is it? *Where is it?*

JIM   What?

GARLAND   The release, the manual release. There isn't
           one! There should be one right there! Who
           put this place together?! Fuck!

> *GARLAND runs back to the wall switch and*
> *flicks it again several times, culminating in a*
> *punch. He stands still a moment trying to*
> *compose himself.*

JIM   What?

GARLAND   You guys see any batteries for this thing
           anywhere?

STUART   No.

JIM   No.

GARLAND   Well *look around!* Maybe it's just the wiring,
           maybe the remote will still work. I'll see
           what I can do about the automatic opener up
           top. Otherwise, if I can't fix it, and you don't
           find some batteries, then later tomorrow or
           the next day or whenever, the good folks
           who own this place are going to come home
           and find *us*, still sitting here, our thumbs up
           our asses. You stupid, *stupid* sonofabitch.
           You've managed to do something I've never
           even heard of. We're trapped inside
           somebody's *garage*, and if that doesn't qualify

us for the All-Canadian Weiney Hall of
Fame, I don't know what will!

JIM   I'm sorry. I lost my temper.

GARLAND   Well, I guess so.

JIM   Try repacking them again.

              JIM hands the remote to STUART.

GARLAND   Gimme a boost up.

JIM   Why? What are you doing?

GARLAND   I'm going to look at these wires. See if I can
              fix'em.

JIM   Right.

GARLAND   Gimme a hand!

              *GARLAND climbs up and dangles near the
              wiring.*

GARLAND   How hard can it be? Like, there's a coupl'a
              wires loose, or something like that.

JIM   What do you know about wires?

GARLAND   I've hot wired a car. Ya, sure — here's some
              wires right here. So all I have to do is reach
              in—

              *He is suddenly electrocuted. A blue spark
              jumps off his hand and he stiffens.*

GARLAND   Ya!

JIM   Christ!

              GARLAND drops to the floor.

STUART   Garland!

JIM   Are you okay?

       Pause.

GARLAND   What?

       GARLAND stands up.

STUART   Are you okay?

GARLAND   Yea. Sure.

       He shakes his head.

GARLAND   I think we're going to have to find some
       other way of getting out though.

       *They stand a moment, not knowing quite
       what to do. Then GARLAND retreats to the
       rear of the garage.*

JIM   What are you doing?

GARLAND   I've got to think. I'm having a smoke break.

JIM   Oh.

STUART   Oh.

       *Both STUART and JIM join GARLAND. All
       three sit on the work table.*

JIM   Gimme a light.

       *STUART lends JIM his lighter. JIM returns
       the lighter after lighting his smoke. STUART
       lights his smoke, but finds the flame has been
       turned up to flame thrower lengths by JIM.
       He is startled, and JIM enjoys a quick chuckle
       at his expense. They all smoke and have a
       reflective moment.*

GARLAND   Fuck.

JIM   Yea. No kidding.

               Pause.

STUART   Yea.

               *Another pause. GARLAND retrieves the
               remote control. He presses the button.
               Nothing.*

GARLAND   Yea, that sucker's good and dead now.
               What'd you do before, Stuart?

STUART   I already tried it.

               Pause. They smoke in silence.

JIM   You think there's any other, you know...

GARLAND   What?

JIM   Secret compartment kind'a things.

GARLAND   Secret compartment?

JIM   Yea.

GARLAND   What are you talking about? There are no
               secret compartments here, okay?

JIM   What's that?

GARLAND   That's a *cabinet.*

JIM   Well?

GARLAND   Well what? It's not secret.

JIM   Why not?

GARLAND   It's right there where you can see it. Can you
               see it?

JIM   Yea.

GARLAND   So how's it secret?

JIM   It's gotta lock on it and everything.

GARLAND   That doesn't make it *secret*.

JIM   You can't tell what's in it.

GARLAND   We don't know what's in it, numb nuts,
                 because we don't know what's in *anything*,
                 because we're ripping the joint off.

JIM   So?

GARLAND   So that's not *secret*, like it's not a *secret*—

JIM   Yea.

GARLAND   *No!* It's like, you don't know what's in
                 someone's house from the street—

JIM   Cause it's secret.

GARLAND   *No!* Cause it's *private*. There's a difference.

JIM   What difference?

GARLAND   Secret and private.

JIM   I don't get the difference. (*to STUART*) Do
                 you get the difference?

STUART   The guy's not hiding things, he's keeping
                 them safe.

GARLAND   Exactly. Like his wife *knows* there're tools
                 out here, he's just keeping them locked up.

JIM   Suddenly you know this guy's wife?

GARLAND   I'm just saying for instance.

JIM   Has *she* got a key?

GARLAND   I don't know! The point is, he's keeping them locked up.

JIM   Why?

GARLAND   So they won't get stolen and stuff.

JIM   Who's going to steal *tools?*

GARLAND   *We are, asshole!* Jesus, you're making me mental!

JIM   I just don't see the difference between secret and private.

GARLAND   Never mind.

JIM   I mean, if something's private, it's also secret.

GARLAND   Never mind!

JIM   I mean, if you go to whack off for instance—

GARLAND   Aw fuck—

JIM   —that's private, *and* it's also secret.

GARLAND   Aw.

JIM   Well? See?

GARLAND   No that's *private*. That's not *secret*.

JIM   How's that not secret?

GARLAND   Everybody knows you whack off, ya Whackoff. I mean, what do you think we think you're doing in the washroom for half an hour?

JIM   But you don't *know* for sure. That makes it *secret* and *private*.

GARLAND   Fine.

JIM   That's all I'm saying.

GARLAND   Fine! And all I'm saying is that this is a garage, Jim, not a pirate cave, not Ali Baba's den, okay?

JIM   Ali who?

GARLAND   Never mind! The thing is this is a *cabinet*, okay? Not buried treasure. You find 'em anywhere, you find 'em in kitchens, okay?

JIM   Okay.

   Slight pause.

   So, you don't think there'd be anything—

GARLAND   NO! What do you think? — You knock on the wall three times and a secret box drops out? Feel under the shelf and suddenly— Hey? What the fuck is this?

   GARLAND finds something under the shelf. He pulls it out — it's a small metal box. He opens it. Music plays. It's a music box.

STUART   It's beautiful.

   The music box stops playing.

JIM   Fuck, that's neat. Why'd the guy put that there?

GARLAND   Don't be stupid. The guy didn't put that there. They probably have a kid. He hid it out here. I used to hide stuff when I was a kid.

STUART   Me too.

JIM   Ya, me too.

> *Pause. GARLAND rewinds the music box,*
> *but only part way. The thing does a couple of*
> *bars of music.*

JIM   Lemme see it a minute. (*as GARLAND hands*
it to him) I wonder how they do all that
stuff.

GARLAND What?

JIM   You know, the wires and stuff.

GARLAND It's not wires. It's springs and latches. It's not
electrical.

JIM   No kidding? It'd be great to know how to do
something like this. (*rewinding it*) I could see
doing that.

GARLAND Right. *You?*

JIM   Yea, I'm good with my hands.

GARLAND Fuck you.

JIM   Fuck you.

GARLAND Let me see it.

> *JIM tucks it in his pocket*

GARLAND Give it back.

JIM   I want to hang onto it for a bit.

GARLAND Give it back.

JIM   Why shouldn't I hold onto it?

GARLAND I found it.

JIM   I found the garage.

GARLAND   Well, we were here first too.

JIM   It's *my* garage opener, isn't it?

GARLAND   Stuart got it to work.

JIM   It's in my pocket, man.

GARLAND   Don't fuck with me.

> *JIM hesitates and suddenly GARLAND explodes, punching him several times in the head, then throwing JIM to the floor on his belly. GARLAND wrenches JIM's arm up behind his back.*

GARLAND   Give it to me!

JIM   You're busting my arm—

GARLAND   Give it to me!

JIM   Ow!

> *GARLAND reaches into JIM's pocket with his other hand and pulls out the music box.*

GARLAND   Now don't you fuck with me anymore.

> *GARLAND stands up.*

JIM   You almost broke my arm.

GARLAND   Well, you wouldn't give it to me.

JIM   I would've given it to you.

GARLAND   Right.

JIM   Now I know whether to trust you or not.

GARLAND   Oh. So that was just a test to see whether you could trust me or not.

JIM   Yea.

GARLAND   So? Did I pass?

JIM   No. You fucken didn't. And that's kind of a
           wanky toy for a guy to have anyway. And I
           was *right*, there *are* secret compartment kinda
           things in here.

GARLAND   Don't start that again.

STUART   We could sand our way through.

JIM   What?

STUART   We could sand our way through. With the
           sanders. Through the wall.

GARLAND   How do you mean?

STUART   We sand a hole in beside the door big enough
           to reach through and unlock it.

GARLAND   How long do you think that would take?

STUART   I don't know. Looks like the garage is home
           made, you know, like the guy built it
           himself. Dead bolts on the door and stuff.
           Depends what he put between the garage
           and the house.

           STUART knocks softly on the walls.

           Coupl'a hours.

JIM   Coupl'a *hours*?

STUART   Maybe less.

JIM   We want to be outta here.

STUART   We can't break through.

GARLAND   There's nothing to pry the door open with.

JIM

You guys are kiddin'? We're going to *sand* our way in?

No objections.

What about the noise?

GARLAND

No one's heard us yet. It's quieter than smashing our way through. Who knows? Maybe people'll just think we're renovating. Come on.

They begin to haul out the sanding equipment.

JIM

Can I see the music box?

GARLAND

No.

JIM

Just for a moment?

GARLAND

No.

STUART

How do you do this?

GARLAND

You wrap the sand paper round here. We re-did one of the group homes once. Sanded everything.

JIM

I just want to look at it.

GARLAND

We're trying to get into the house, okay?

JIM

Okay. Hey!

GARLAND

What?

JIM

There're only two sanders.

GARLAND

Yea.

JIM

What am I supposed to do?

GARLAND

Use a sanding block.

JIM   And do it by *hand?*

GARLAND   Yea.

JIM   Right.

               JIM takes two sanding blocks.

               This is just like kindergarten. We used to get
               these to make music with.

               *He brushes two pieces of sand paper together
               as he hums a quick marching tune. Suddenly
               he stops.*

               Hey!

               No reaction from the others.

               HEY!

GARLAND   What?!

JIM   We haven't looked up there.

GARLAND   Where?

JIM   In the rafters, man.

GARLAND   We can see through 'em.

JIM   There might be something hidden, taped, you
               know? Money, drugs, you know?

GARLAND   People don't hide their money and drugs
               taped to the rafters of fucking garages,
               bonehead. (*to STUART*) We need an extension
               cord.

JIM   Boost me up.

GARLAND   No.

JIM   Just gimme your hand.

GARLAND   I ain't going to boost you up, now quit
                 clowning around.

JIM   (*to STUART*) Boost me up.

STUART   (*backing up*) Your runners are—

JIM   Aw Christ.

                 *JIM quickly kicks off his runners. STUART
                 gives JIM a boost up. JIM, looking extremely
                 ungainly, makes his way into the rafters. Dust
                 comes spilling down. GARLAND brushes the
                 dust and frowns up at JIM.*

GARLAND   Quit screwing around, will you?

STUART   Here's an extension.

                 JIM slips on the rafters.

JIM   Ow! Sonofabitch.

                 *More dust comes spilling down on
                 GARLAND and STUART.*

GARLAND   Oh, man!

JIM   Hey!

                 No reaction.

                 Hey!

GARLAND   What?!

JIM   You said I wouldn't find anything up here —
                 well, prepare to eat your fucking words—

GARLAND   What?

                 *JIM scrambles along the rafters and grabs
                 something.*

JIM   Oh yea.

GARLAND   What?

JIM   Yea, you said I wouldn't find anything. Wait 'til you see this.

GARLAND   What? What is it?

               JIM comes tumbling down and stands up holding a tackle box and a fishing pole.

JIM   This!

               Pause.

GARLAND   A fishing pole.

JIM   But what about *this?*

GARLAND   It's a tackle box.

               No comprehension from JIM.

               You keep your fishing line, hooks and all that in it.

               GARLAND opens it to display shelves full of hooks, spinners, and a fishing hat.

               Haven't you ever been fishing?

JIM   Ya, sure. Lot's of times.

               JIM fingers through the tackle box. Lots of glittering hooks — no drugs or money.

GARLAND   Now, you through messing around? Let's get started.

               STUART has backed into a box of cans.

STUART   Hey. These aren't empty.

GARLAND   What?

STUART   These beer cans.

JIM   You're kiddin'?

STUART   There's six still full.

GARLAND   Okay! Throw me one.

            STUART throws him one.

JIM   And me!

            *STUART tosses him one. JIM and
            GARLAND crack them open and drink.*

JIM   Yes! I could drink about a dozen of these, eh?
               Garland?

GARLAND   What?

JIM   About a dozen?

GARLAND   Yea!

JIM   Ahh! Now that tastes good. To us three in
               Vancouver, eh? Stuart, aren't you going to
               have one?

            *STUART looks at the box, which is damp. He
            rubs his hands against his jeans.*

STUART   Ah. No.

JIM   Okay! More for you and me!

            GARLAND picks up the sanders.

GARLAND   We can trade off every once in a while.
               There's a plug outlet there.

            *STUART plugs both sanders in. GARLAND
            turns his on to test it, then turns it off.*

GARLAND   We have lift off. Let's play some tunes
               while we do it. Fire up the box, Jim.

               *JIM turns on the radio and fiddles with the
               stations.*

JIM   Crap. Crap. Crap.

               He comes upon The Bee Gees.

ALL THREE   Ugh!

               He comes upon something a little harder.

JIM   Okay!

               He cranks it up.

GARLAND   All right. (*to STUART*) So, right about here?

               *He paints an "x" on the wall with a finger
               dipped in beer.*

STUART   Should do it.

GARLAND   Gentlemen, start your engines!

               *They fire up the sanders, take a swig of beer
               and begin. Fade down lights.*

               End of Act One.

Act Two

	Music up. The radio is on, loud. The sanders are also roaring away. Lights up. Everyone is covered with saw dust. STUART and GARLAND continue to sand the wall. There's a patch of about four feet where they've sanded through the dry wall and fibre glass insulation and are now sanding through wood. JIM has a fisherman's hat on and is practicing casting to the end of the garage.
JIM	Yaa!
	The fishing line goes whizzing to the end of the garage, thumping against a box.
JIM	It jumps!
	He reels in the line.
	He clubs it, and *in it goes*! Into the basket, another be-yootiful lake trout.
	He goes to cast again, but accidentally releases the line early and it ends up on GARLAND's shoulder. GARLAND tugs on the line and JIM turns around.
GARLAND	Watch what you're doing.
JIM	Okay.
	GARLAND returns to his work.
JIM	How much longer do you figure? Garland?

GARLAND doesn't hear.

JIM   Gar?

*GARLAND still doesn't hear. JIM casts
again...*

Yaaa ... ow.

*...but this time he gets the hook snagged on
the back of his head. He winces and tries to get
it out. He can't.*

*He tries to lay the fishing rod down. It falls
and the hook tugs against his head. He is
forced to call for help.*

JIM   Hey! Hey!

GARLAND   What?!

JIM   I'm snagged.

GARLAND   What?

*GARLAND turns off his sander, as does
STUART.*

JIM   I'm snagged. On the back of my head.

GARLAND turns down the music.

GARLAND   Yea. I guess you are. He's snagged on ... looks
                    to be, the back of his head, Stu.

JIM   I can't get it out.

GARLAND   No, I guess you can't.

JIM   Give me a hand.

GARLAND lights up a cigarette.

GARLAND   Well, Stu, it looks like Jim finally caught himself a big one.

JIM   Quit messing around, will ya?

GARLAND   "Quit *messing around*, will ya?" Where have I heard that one before? Eh? Stu? *Where* have I heard that before? (*to JIM*) Hey, you gonna fry this one up as it is, Jim, or fillet it?

JIM   Aw go fuck yourself.

           GARLAND tugs on the line..

JIM   Ow.

GARLAND   Ah, ah, ah. There's one rule all the real fishermen obey, Jim, and you know what that is?

           He tugs on the line again.

JIM   Ow.

GARLAND   I said, you know what that is?

           He tugs.

JIM   Ow. *What?*

GARLAND   It's almost like a lesson of life. Never, ever—

JIM   Ow.

GARLAND   —tell anyone to *fuck themselves*, when you have a fish hook planted—

           Tug.

JIM   Ow.

GARLAND   —in the back of your head. So ... what do you want me to do about this fish hook?

JIM   Can you get it out somehow?

GARLAND   Hm, hm, hm.

> *GARLAND tries sliding it out.*

JIM   Ow.

GARLAND   Nope, that doesn't work. Well. I could try *cutting* it out. Or, I suppose we could *sand* it out—

JIM   Quit screwing around.

GARLAND   Or, I suppose the easiest thing, would be to just pull—

> *He pulls it out with a short, sharp tug.*

JIM   *Ow!*

GARLAND   —it out.

JIM   You sonofabitch.

GARLAND   If you weren't screwing around all the time!

JIM   There're only two sanders! What'm I sposed to do? It's stupid to do it by hand. You can't sand your way through a freakin' wall by hand.

GARLAND   Ya, right.

JIM   I'll do my share when we get in.

GARLAND   What's that?

JIM   What's what?

GARLAND   Your share?

JIM   I'll lift stuff.

GARLAND   You'll lift stuff?

JIM   I'm good at lifting stuff. I worked for a
           furniture moving company for a while, used
           to move fridges, sofas, stoves, everything.
           And like, they showed you how to pack
           stuff. You know, you could fit almost
           everything in this house and garage into the
           back of a single pick up truck if you only
           knew how to position it right. It's like a
           science. (*pulling out a cigarette*) Gimme a
           light.

GARLAND   Ask Stuart.

JIM   You are so cheap.

GARLAND   Bite me. I only have a couple of matches
           left. Ask Stuart, he's got the lighter.

JIM   Gimme a light.

           *STUART passes his butane lighter over. JIM
           lights up, then passes the lighter back.*

JIM   Tell me the truth, how come you brought him
           along?

GARLAND   I thought he'd be useful.

JIM   Ya, right. Like he's really helped us *break
           in*.

GARLAND   At least he hasn't *snagged* himself on a
           freaking fish hook. God, this dust gets up
           your nose and into your eyes.

JIM   You said after we did this place and got
           some money, we'd go to the coast and all
           that. We still going to do all that?

GARLAND   Why not? Sell the stuff, party, and then find
           our own way after that. You know?

JIM   Right, yea. Sure.

> *Pause.*

JIM   So, what're you going to do?

GARLAND   I don't know.

> *Pause.*

JIM   So, it's a secret?

GARLAND   *I don't know.* Let me spell it for you: I for I, don't for don't, know for know! I can't tell you what I haven't figured out yet. It's not a secret. A secret is something you know, but you're not telling, but I don't know! Okay?!

JIM   Okay.

> *Pause.*

JIM   So, it's private?

GARLAND   *Fuck!*

> *GARLAND moves away from JIM.*

JIM   How much longer?

STUART   We're through the layer this side. Looks like we have another layer of wood to go on the other.

JIM   Lemme see that music box a minute.

GARLAND   No.

JIM   Just for a minute.

GARLAND   No.

JIM   I'm not going to do anything with it.

Pause. JIM goes over to the empty bottles.

JIM　　　　　Nothing ... left.

He checks the other empties.

JIM　　　　　Nothing. Nothing. Nothing left. You know what is too fucking bad? Garland?

GARLAND　　No, what?

JIM　　　　　It's too fucking bad that the car wasn't here, eh? Then we could've, you know, simply loaded all the stuff into the trunk, and driven off. Driven right off to Vancouver. That'd be okay, eh? Pull out, everything in the trunk, and *vrooom*, all the way to the coast, eh?

GARLAND　　Right, Jim. That'd be perfect. That'd be *right on*. Wouldn't that be *right on*, Stu? If the car was *here* when we walked in? Right *here*. Wouldn't that be perfect?

JIM　　　　　What's so stupid about that?

GARLAND　　Think about it.

JIM　　　　　Well?

GARLAND　　Nothing.

JIM　　　　　But what?

GARLAND　　Just *think* about it.

JIM　　　　　I have!

GARLAND　　You don't see, do you? If the car is here ... then?

Brief pause.

JIM　　　　　Then?

GARLAND	Yea, *then*?
JIM	Then what? What's he talking about? Do you know what he's talking about? What are you talking about?
GARLAND	Forget it!
JIM	What?
GARLAND	If the car is here, then what is here?
JIM	The car alarm?
GARLAND	No! If the car is here, then...?

Long pause.

JIM	What, the car shampoo, the interior vacuuming kit, *what?*
GARLAND	*The car owners*! The *car owners* are here, and if the car owners are here, then we aren't, God use your head!
JIM	Whoooo. He's touchy, eh? The *car owners.* The *car owners.* Well, maybe the car owners are here, but maybe they, you know, go for a walk. People go for walks. Maybe they're out ... biking. Maybe they go someplace by cab, even people with cars take a cab every once—
GARLAND	Maybe they're out chewing gum, watching the movies, playing cards and screwing the dog all at the same time! *Maybe* they just own a car so they can park it in here all the time and just look out the door every once in a while to make sure it's still there: "That car you bought that we *never, ever drive* anywhere still parked out back in the garage dear?" '*Kay? Is that what you want to believe???*

>*Silence while GARLAND finishes slipping a new piece of sand paper into his machine.*

JIM
>That's all I'm saying. The car could, you know, be out here.

>*GARLAND glares at JIM and starts up his sander. STUART is still trying to fix sand paper to his sander. STUART lights a cigarette at this point and JIM has once again left the flame turned up to flame thrower proportions.*

STUART
>Ah!

>*STUART drops the lighter, and glances over at JIM. JIM wanders over to the work bench where he plays with the vice, taps on the lid of a paint can, then pries the top off a container of paint thinner. He bends over it and inhales.*

JIM
>I'm not as stupid as you think. You know. Gar. What about that dog?

GARLAND
>What about *what* dog?

JIM
>That dog outside, started to bark? I got it to be quiet.

>*He sniffs some more.*

>You notice that? Gar? I got a way with dogs. I used to train dogs. You got to *think* like the dog. That's the trick.

>*He takes another sniff.*

>You want a sniff?

STUART
>What?

JIM
>(*sniffing*) You want some?

STUART
>No.

JIM   Ever tried it?

STUART   No.

JIM   It's okay. Cheap buzz.

> *He inhales some more. A piece of sand paper goes ripping off GARLAND's sander.*

GARLAND   Shit. Where's that other— (*turning*) What are you doing?

> *JIM stares at GARLAND but does not reply. GARLAND glances at STUART.*

GARLAND   You going to do that?

STUART   No.

GARLAND   (*to JIM*) You're not going to be much use "lifting stuff" outta the house if you're high.

JIM   No problem. I been wrecked dozens of times and the cops come in, and I'm the only one able to get my shit together.

GARLAND   On paint thinner?

JIM   All kinds'a shit. I don't have to do it now, I mean, I can do it later. After.

GARLAND   We sell some stuff and we can buy some booze after. Or some grass.

JIM   Yea. Sure.

> *GARLAND turns and JIM sniffs some more.*

GARLAND   Where's that other piece of sandpaper?

JIM   What?

GARLAND   That other piece of sandpaper you had? Where is it?

JIM   I don't know.

GARLAND   (*turning the radio down*) What do you mean,
               you don't know?

JIM   I forget.

GARLAND   It can only be in so many places. Where did
               you have it last?

JIM   I don't know.

GARLAND   How can you lose something in a garage?

JIM   *You* find it then.

GARLAND   Where were you sitting?

               *GARLAND goes to one place and searches
               through the debris.*

GARLAND   Here?

               He goes to another place.

               Here?

               He throws aside some of the debris.

               We've spent the first hour getting in to this
               garage, and the last coupl'a hours trying to
               get out, we're wasting time, now where is it?!

               Pause.

JIM   Where's the music box?

               Pause.

GARLAND   Why?

JIM   Can I look at it? For a minute?

> *GARLAND stares at JIM for a long moment,*
> *then withdraws it from his jacket and sets it*
> *on the work table. JIM picks it up.*

JIM   It's over there, under the cardboard box.

> *GARLAND retrieves the sandpaper. JIM picks*
> *up the music box. Gives it a little bit of a wind*
> *up and listens to it.*

JIM   Stu going to Vancouver too? Gar? Gar? (*to*
         STUART) You going to Vancouver too?

STUART   I think so.

JIM   That right, Gar? Gar? Gar?

GARLAND Yea!

JIM   The way I figure it, we ought to kinda hang
         out together when we get there, for a little
         while anyway, you know? I know places we
         could do. (*to STUART*) You know Vancouver?

STUART   No.

JIM   It's fucking *big*, man. A lot of fucking people.
         You gotta know your way round.

> *He sniffs more thinner.*

Everything's bigger. The downtown. The
night scene. The ocean. That's a lotta fucking
water.

GARLAND I thought you'd never been to the coast?

JIM   I been to the coast.

Just not recently, like not in the last coupl'a
years, but me and a cousin I got out there, we
used to get together in the summer and raise
shit, we used to — fuck, do *everything!* We
picked up these two chicks? Out near the

                      downtown? And we went out on a fishing boat? Got wrecked and screwed these two, right there, on the deck of this boat. Right there. Right on the deck.

GARLAND   When?

JIM   When what?

GARLAND   When's the last time you were out to Vancouver?

JIM   I don't know. Maybe five years ago, but it's not like the city's changed a lot since then—

GARLAND   So you were, eleven years old when you fucked these two out on the boat?

JIM   I never said it was the *last* time we were out that this happened.

GARLAND   So, at *most*, eleven years old.

JIM   Well ah, I'm not sure ... about how *exact*, five years. Maybe I was a little older.

GARLAND   Where'd you learn to steer a boat?

JIM   I never said I drove it.

GARLAND   You just let it drift?

JIM   I rented it. They got guys who'll do that stuff for you.

GARLAND   You rented it?

JIM   Ya, I rented it, what the fuck are you, the cops?

GARLAND   For how much?

JIM   I don't know, it was a while back—

GARLAND   Five years ago? Wasn't that when your step
             dad was wailin' on you? So, what? He just
             took out a wad'a cash, said "Jim, go rent a
             boat?"

JIM   He didn't know 'bout it.

GARLAND   How much was the deposit for this boat?

JIM   Don't know.

GARLAND   You don't know. Must'a been a whack'a
             dough for them to let you fuck a coupl'a
             eleven year olds out on the deck. Kind of a
             Love Boat for elementary school kids, eh?

             Slight pause

             You are so fulla shit.

JIM   Gimme another smoke.

             STUART passes JIM a smoke.

             I need a light too.

             *STUART passes him his lighter. JIM lights up
             and returns the lighter.*

             I *been* to Vancouver. Don't you worry about
             that. I may mess around with some of the
             details—

GARLAND   Details!

JIM   —to make a story interesting, but I've been to
             Vancouver. It's not like *you've* never told a
             lie. I mean, you'd have to be stupid not to lie
             sometimes. *You've* lied.

STUART   Sure.

JIM   Sure you have. Who hasn't? You gotta lie to
             get through some shit. Be crazy not to lie.

He takes a sander.

Gimme that. I'll take a shift. Christ, all the stories we've heard in group, you know everyone of us has lied, but I'm not stupid. It's me who got us in here. Me who found out when it'd be empty. Me. I'm good at making plans. Before I ended up at the Home I didn't get caught for nearly three years. How long after did you get caught?

STUART   A year.

JIM   And *you* got ratted on within a couple'a weeks.

GARLAND   I wanted to get caught.

JIM   Ya, right. You *wanted* to get caught. Why?

No answer.

Why?

GARLAND   Look, it's beyond you.

JIM   You wanted to get caught?

GARLAND   Yea, I wanted to get caught! Just let—

JIM   Hey! I may not be a genius in some ways, but I'm sharp enough to figure out that no one ever *wants* to get caught, okay?

Slight pause.

My first psychiatrist said I had an excellent mind for planning things. For instance, you take what I did after this guy dropped his remote. Gar tell you about that?

STUART reaches for the sander.

STUART   You want me to sand?

JIM   Naw. I'll do it. In a minute.

JIM   I take the wrong bus back from my parole
             officer's — not my fault, the knob of the bus
             driver got the wrong number up in the
             window like a fucking decoy — anyway, I'm
             walking back, and I see this guy backing out
             of his garage—

             Throughout this, JIM pries open a can of paint
             and begins dabbling with it.

             —and he runs over this garbage can, so he
             gets out to move it, and he drops the remote,
             and I see it. So, I keep real cool, and just
             hang out and sure enough he hops back into
             his car and fucks off. *I pick up the remote.* I
             could'a gone in right then, but ... no, I figure,
             get some guys and come back on the long
             weekend when you can do it right.

             He paints his nose.

             (*to GARLAND*) I didn't have to tell you, you
             know?

             (*he daubs some streaks on his cheek, then, to*
             STUART) When did he tell you?

STUART   A week ago.

JIM   A week ago? Seems like plenty of time to
             tell me you'd told Stuart.

             GARLAND ignores JIM who playfully picks
             up a paint brush, dips it and pretends to be
             about to paint STUART.

STUART   No. I don't like it.

JIM   (*to GARLAND*) Why didn't you tell me?
             Gar? Why didn't you tell me?

GARLAND   I forgot, look is *someone* else going to sand?

JIM   I'm gonna.

GARLAND   "I'm gonna."

       He turns and sees JIM's painted face.

       Will you quit screwing the dog and get over here? You better not sniff anymore, you're fucked up enough as it is.

JIM   Don't tell me what to do.

       JIM takes a deep sniff of thinner.

       I organized this. Don't tell me.

STUART   Can I have that?

JIM   Take it.

       He tosses the sander to STUART.

       Don't act like you're the brains of this outfit. *I'm* the brains. *I'm* the brains, and you know what you are? You know what you are?

       JIM turns and drops his pants.

       You know what you are? Garland? You know what you are? *Garland?*

GARLAND   Fuck! What?

       GARLAND turns, sees JIM's raised bum and JIM convulsed with laughter. He quickly reaches over, grabs the paint brush and smucks paint on JIM's bare bum.

JIM   Oh funny! Really funny.
       Then he makes a discovery.

       Hey!

He backs up against the wall of the garage and leaves a print of his naked butt.

Hey, look! Garland, look! Hey, look! Look!

GARLAND   What now?

GARLAND turns and stares.

Excellent. I didn't know you could do a self portrait.

JIM   Cool, eh?

He backs up against the wall again.

GARLAND   Aw, don't go printing your butt all over the walls.

JIM   Why?

JIM applies another coat of paint and starts backing up against the walls.

The police got our bum prints on file? That it, Garland? They're going to track us down by matching *bum* prints? Well, let (*making a print*) them (*making another*) try.

He makes a print, and pulls his pants back up again. He draws a happy face on one of the prints.

Kinda looks like you, don't you think?

Both STUART and GARLAND are ignoring him again.

(*taking the sander from STUART*) Gimme that.

GARLAND   Fuck! Will you cut it out!

JIM   I'm gonna sand!

GARLAND   You been screwing around, screwing around,
           screwing around ever since we got here. If you
           can't get it together *here*, for like, a couple'a
           hours, why the *fuck* would I want to hang
           around with you in Vancouver? Now gimme
           the fucking music box!

           He takes the music box from JIM.

           And *sand* if you're gonna sand.

           GARLAND turns away from JIM.

JIM   I was *gonna* sand.

           Slight pause.

           What do you mean by that? You mean we're
           not going to hang out together in Vancouver?
           That what you mean?

           No answer.

           We been doing this, what? Two hours? We're
           wasting our time trying to come through, I
           mean, it's gotta be just about like tissue paper
           now. All it needs is a good shot now. Like—

           *JIM slams the wall with his sander and the
           handle comes off it. GARLAND turns his
           sander off.*

GARLAND   Some tissue paper.

JIM   I felt it give.

GARLAND   The sander? Too fucking right.

JIM   I suppose you're going to blame me for this
           now?

GARLAND   Why would I do that? It's the fucking wall
           that jumped up and broke the sander, isn't it?

JIM   Sander's a cheap piece'a shit—

GARLAND   Right.

JIM   —and, I'm telling you, I could feel the wall
           start to give.

GARLAND   Right. It's just about transparent.

JIM   I could put my head through it if I wanted.

GARLAND   Right.

JIM   You don't think I could? You don't think I
           could?

GARLAND   Why not? It's for sure the hardest part'a
           your body.

           *JIM smacks the wall with his head, surprising
           both GARLAND and STUART.*

GARLAND   Go easy, man. We don't want the whole
           garage tumbling down round us.

           JIM smacks the wall even harder.

GARLAND   Take it easy.

JIM   I'm coming through, man.

           He smacks it harder.

           It's starting to give.

STUART   Jim.

GARLAND   Settle down, Jim.

           JIM smacks it even harder.

JIM   I hear it cracking!

               *JIM smashes the wall with his head. He
               stands still a moment.*

STUART   Jim?

GARLAND   You okay? Jim?

               JIM drops to the floor. Blackout.

               End of Act Two.

Act Three

Lights up. The wall has been sanded through, finally, and the garage door to the house is now open. JIM lies on the floor of the garage, bathed in the light from the house. STUART sits on the steps leading into the house, and stares at JIM.

GARLAND   Here you go.

GARLAND enters and tosses STUART a watch. STUART glances at it, seems to like it, puts it on. GARLAND shakes his wet hair, sprinkling drops on STUART.

STUART   Don't.

GARLAND   Shower was good, man. Got rid of all that dust.

GARLAND stares at JIM, then walks over to him and crouches beside him.

GARLAND   Wake up.

He slaps JIM lightly on the face.

Wake up.

No reaction.

Tsk.

GARLAND takes a drink from a bottle of wine he's taken from the fridge inside the house.

GARLAND   What time is it?

STUART   Four.

GARLAND   I'm beat. Here.

            GARLAND tosses STUART his towel.

            Towel me off.

            *GARLAND stretches out and places his head
            on STUART's lap. STUART dries
            GARLAND's hair.*

STUART   What are we going to do?

GARLAND   I'll give him a couple more minutes.

STUART   You hungry?

GARLAND   Gimme some of that meat.

            *STUART hands GARLAND a garlic coil
            that's on the floor next to him. STUART, by
            himself, is methodically and in order of the
            ones he likes best, eating an entire box of
            chocolates.*

GARLAND   How can you eat all those?

STUART   They're good. What you said about the
            coast...

GARLAND   Yea?

STUART   Is that the way it is? Going our own way?

GARLAND   For him, yea. Not for us. Come on – (*looping
            an arm around STUART's leg and giving it an
            affectionate squeeze*) — we're a team, right?
            But, I mean, look at him. "I hear it
            cracking." It's a wonder he can dress himself,
            his brain's that tiny. Poor bastard. Face it,
            you can't do a thing with him. I mean, even

breaking into a garage, which shouldn't be a big test of your social skills, is like, beyond him. (*hacking off a piece of the coil and popping it into his mouth*) See, I got no issue with the recovery program back at group, you know — except it's not for me, not anymore. Not for me or you. But, like, I can at least appreciate that the therapy they did helped me when I first came in. You gotta move on, and like you and me, we have. You gotta realize what a nowhere life you had if you want to change it. Right?

STUART   Sure.

GARLAND   See, *you* understand. I would never have fucking lived without the help I got, but now I'm ready to get out, like you. But *this* horse cock (*gesturing to JIM*) thinks there's nothing wrong with him now and never was. A week in Vancouver and the heat'll pick him up. He'll be prowling the playgrounds, dorking some seven year old in a park.

(*taking a swig of his wine*) When I was hooking, I used to see guys like him all the time. A couple'a years from now, he doesn't get his shit together, he's going to be a very scary dude.

STUART   He's pretty scary now.

GARLAND   Give him a few more years and a couple'a terms in the pen and see how scary he gets.

     STUART sticks his finger into one of the chocolates and considers it.

STUART   It's cherry. You want it?

GARLAND   No. Jim?

     No reaction.

GARLAND   *Jim?*

                   Still nothing.

                   Tsk. Ya, when we get to Vancouver, you and me, right?

STUART   Right.

GARLAND   A new start. We can hang out with a couple'a friends I've got out there 'til we get our legs. Get a job landscaping to begin with. I done that before. Lotta big yards out there. Lotta grass to be cut. Then, if we get lucky, you know what?

STUART   What?

GARLAND   It's just a thought, like something I been thinking about. No promises or anything. But, you know, it's a possibility.

                   Pause.

STUART   Right? What?

                   Pause.

GARLAND   Movies.

                   Pause.

STUART   Movies?

GARLAND   Yea.

                   Pause.

STUART   You mean look at them?

GARLAND   No! It's just like Hollywood out there. They're making films all the time. Why not with us?

STUART   Don't you have to know how to ... act, or
                anything?

GARLAND   No, no, no, it's not like that in film. You
                don't have to act. It's *film!* It's like they've
                got jobs just to *stand around*.

STUART   No way.

GARLAND   Yea! Like, stand ins — that's what they call
                it — and all you gotta do is hang out, cause
                they don't want to pay Stars to just hang out,
                right? Hanging out they can get anyone to do.
                They save Stars for the heavy shit, you
                know, the tough acting stuff, when they
                have to cry or kiss or die or whatever. It's
                just like baseball and designated hitters.
                Right?

STUART   So, just, walk around like?

GARLAND   Yea. Start out as, kinda stand ins, and then
                — who knows? Eventually, maybe something
                more. I mean, Christ, the way I heard it
                James Dean was just some kinda street kid
                with an attitude before he got his first gig
                and look where he went.

                GARLAND glances over at STUART who
                obviously has no idea who James Dean was or
                where he went.

GARLAND   Nevermind. Anyway, the thing is we could
                be doing stuff like that instead of, you know,
                stuff like this.

STUART   It sounds ... too easy.

GARLAND   Maybe that's just to us. Maybe that's the
                way it's *supposed* to be, you know? In real
                life. Easy? Instead of always fucked up and
                turned inside out. Why not easy? I could use
                a little bit of easy. You could use a little bit
                of easy. Easy sounds all right to me.

STUART	Walk around. I could do that.
GARLAND	Sure you could. And like, there's other stuff too, carrying the cameras and cables and things like that. There's a lotta that shit.
STUART	Any'a that'd be great. Movies, eh?
GARLAND	Yea.
STUART	So, you really think it's going to work out?
GARLAND	Yea, I do. I really do. No more'a this shit. Knocking some place over for a couple'a hundred bucks. No more group homes, someone always telling you what to do, when you can use the shower, who you can see. Some douche bucket freaking out and puttin' his fist, or *head* through a wall or a window. No running off just to hang out on the street or in somebody's mother's basement and sleep on the floor. A new start, right? Together, you and me. (*giving STUART a little punch*) Maybe we'll even get a place of our own.
STUART	*That'd* be decent.
GARLAND	Wouldn't it? Like, not right away, but eventually, eh?
STUART	With a ... balcony, even.
GARLAND	Why not? View of the city.
STUART	View of the mountains.
GARLAND	Maybe even a view of the ocean.
STUART	Of the ocean?
GARLAND	Yea.
STUART	Don't think I'd like that.

GARLAND   Well, it wouldn't have to be of the ocean.
           But a place of our own where nobody knows
           us, except as *us*. No case histories or any'a
           that. Just us.

           STUART eats a chocolate.

STUART   That'd be great. Maybe we should just go.
           Now.

GARLAND   You mean, and leave him here? Like this?

STUART   Yea.

GARLAND   Uh uh.

STUART   Why not?

GARLAND   I don't think the bastard's really hurt. I
           think he just had too much thinner, but ...
           you know, I mean, if he were to puke and
           choke after we left ... and died. We could be
           charged. And they'll *find* you for murder,
           Vancouver or whereever.

STUART   You think so?

GARLAND   Oh yea. Eventually. (*as STUART takes
           another chocolate*) Eat something healthier,
           for Chrissake.

STUART   I've got some Oreos in my pocket for later.

           GARLAND stands.

GARLAND   Jim!

           *No reaction from JIM. GARLAND turns his
           attention back to STUART.*

           Come on. Let's load up the bikes and the
           backpacks. If he's still out when we finish
           we'll try dragging him to the shower.

> *GARLAND picks up a backpack and walks inside. STUART looks at JIM, steps close to him. For a moment he stares down at JIM, then touches him with the toe of his runner. GARLAND returns with his backpack loaded. He's stuffing a video camera inside it. STUART is still staring at JIM.*

STUART   Garland? Maybe we *should* just leave him.

GARLAND   What?

STUART   Maybe we should just go.

GARLAND   Uh uh. We've got to get him out of *here* at least.

> *GARLAND tosses STUART a backpack.*

Fill this.

> *He goes to the radio.*

Tunes while we work.

> *He turns on the radio. Soft music filters in.*

Come on. Let's go.

STUART   I did my old man, you know?

> *GARLAND keeps packing.*

You hear me?

GARLAND   Yea, I heard you. I knew that already.

STUART   You did?

GARLAND   Yea. I think most of us kinda suspected.

STUART   Who?

GARLAND   The rest'a the group.

STUART	You're kidding?
GARLAND	Look. I know you're pretty closed mouth and all, but you let some stuff go. You told us he beat you up, you told us your uncle did you, give us some credit, I think a lot of us kinda put two and two together and figured you musta done your old man too.
STUART	What do you mean?
GARLAND	I mean we knew already, Stu.
STUART	Knew what?
GARLAND	That you did your old man.

GARLAND hoists a bag up into the bike's carrier.

STUART	I don't think you get me.
GARLAND	Stuart, I *get* you.
STUART	I mean I really did my old man.
GARLAND	So did I. Okay?

Pause.

STUART	I don't mean I had sex with him. I mean, that too. I mean I killed him.

Pause.

GARLAND	Are you shittin' me?
STUART	No.

GARLAND turns off the radio.

GARLAND	You mean you killed your Dad?
STUART	Yea.

Pause.

GARLAND   How?

STUART   He was out camping and he'd picked me up. I wasn't supposed to be there. No one knew. He'd do that kind of stuff, sometimes. Arrange secret meetings and all that. He was going to drop me back at my Aunty's, that's where I was for the weekend. He got drinking and passed out and I...

          Slight pause.

          There was a stream that went past the camp site. He was close to it, where he passed out was close to it. I thought it wouldn't be very hard to kinda roll him in.

          Pause.

GARLAND   So, you did?

          STUART nods.

STUART   He didn't go in very deep. He just lay there, on his belly, face down, breathin' water. I sat on the picnic table for a coupla hours, rollin' cigarettes, watching him. Then I walked back to the highway and hitched a ride into town.

GARLAND   And nobody said anything?

STUART   I kept thinking someone would, but nobody was waiting for him especially and they didn't even start a search until a week later. When the cops found him, I don't think anyone looked really close at what had happened. Just another drunk passed out and drowned.

GARLAND   You didn't tell anyone?

> *STUART shakes his head.*

STUART   I kept expecting ... to feel something, to feel ... you know? But I never did. People would talk about Dad and I'd find myself getting real quiet. And I just kept getting quieter and quieter. That was four years ago. Nobody even thinks anything about it anymore.

GARLAND   But you do? Think about it?

STUART   Yea. I do.

> *GARLAND resumes packing, and then stops.*

GARLAND   You're not shitting me on this, this isn't just some B.S...?

STUART   No.

> *GARLAND stares at STUART.*

GARLAND   Cause if you are...

> *STUART stares back at GARLAND.*

GARLAND   That's a hell of a story.

> *GARLAND slowly begins packing again.*

GARLAND   And you're sure you haven't told anyone?

STUART   Uh uh.

GARLAND   How come you haven't told anyone?

STUART   They're sending guys like me up to adult court to serve adult time. I don't want that.

> *Pause.*

GARLAND   Quit eating the chocolates!

STUART   You want some?

GARLAND   No! (*running a hand through his hair*) Well, that's a fuck of a thing to find out now. You should've told someone.

STUART   I told you.

GARLAND   Yea. Well. Sooner. And someone besides me.

STUART   What difference does it make?

GARLAND   What difference does it make?

STUART   You're the only one who knows.

GARLAND   That's not the thing! It's an *inside* kinda thing, it's what I was talking about. Earlier. It's what I was just saying to you a couple'a minutes ago.

    Slight pause.

Look. Look, this is something you can think about when we get out to the coast. It's just... I've said a lotta shit about the therapists and counsellors and alla those guys, and you know, I'll give you that a lot, you know, most, even, of what happens in therapy is BS, but ah ... I mean, if you had seen me when I was first brought in to the program you would not have believed me. I was so, totally, completely fucked up, I mean I was ... I couldn't have told you what the truth was if you had tattooed it on my balls, I made *him* look like a Quaker—

STUART   A what?

GARLAND   Nevermind. It's ... it's ah ... Just take my word for it, I was fucked up. In so many ways. And the big thing that helped me was ... that I told this therapist—

STUART   I told *you.*

GARLAND But that's not enough, I mean, *she* helped me, you know, to put my head back together.

STUART I can't do that.

GARLAND I'm not saying you have to—

STUART I can't do it, that's all—

GARLAND Don't get excited—

STUART I can't tell one of them.

GARLAND Just *think* about it. That's all I'm saying. Think about it. I mean, you don't have to do anything, not right this minute, so ... just think about it. Okay?

STUART Okay. But...

GARLAND What?

STUART I told *you*. That's something, right?

GARLAND Yea. That's something.

STUART And we're still going to Vancouver, right? You and me?

GARLAND Yea. Sure.

  JIM stirs, opens his eyes, and wakes. He rises, looking slightly dazed, goes to the paint thinner and has a sniff.

JIM Ah.

  He sniffs again.

  Okay.

GARLAND You all right?

JIM Fine.

He sniffs again.

GARLAND   You should probably take it easy after
           bashing your head up like that. Jim?

JIM   You know, you sound exactly like my stepdad
           when you say that. "Don't do this, don't do
           that, watch what you're doing, you should
           probably take it easy." Well, I don't feel
           like taking it easy...

           He sniffs again.

GARLAND   Come on, we got a bunch of stuff. We've got
           to get going.

JIM   Yea?

GARLAND   Your plan *worked* man, we're loaded.

JIM   Is any of the stuff good?

STUART   Good chocolates.

GARLAND   Video camera, camera, couple'a watches,
           some rings and stuff. A hundred bucks and
           change, and ... credit cards.

JIM   Okay! Lemme see 'em.

           GARLAND shows them to JIM.

GARLAND   But we can only use'em around here. Then we
           dump'em. We don't want anyone to be able to
           trace where we've gone.

JIM   Fair enough. So, we did okay?

GARLAND   Yea, we did okay.

JIM   Maybe you should reconsider then.

GARLAND   'Bout what?

JIM   About Vancouver, now that everything's gone
               so well. 'Bout me and Vancouver.

GARLAND   Let's get outta here first, then we'll talk
               about that.

               JIM stares at GARLAND for a moment.

JIM   Gimme a drink.

               *GARLAND hands JIM the bottle. JIM grabs
               GARLAND's wrist and hangs onto it.*

               You're sure?

               *GARLAND pulls his arm away. JIM drinks
               from the bottle.*

GARLAND   If you want to look around real quick to see if
               there's anything else you want to take—

JIM   I heard, you know.

               Pause.

GARLAND   Heard what?

JIM   'Bout his old man.

               Pause.

GARLAND   So? You heard about his old man.

STUART   Are you going to tell?

JIM   I don't know. Are we hanging out when we
               get to the coast? Or what?

GARLAND   You going to tell if we aren't?

               JIM drinks again, then laughs.

JIM   Changes everything, doesn't it? Hey? Stuart?
               Garland? Changes *everything*.

> *He laughs again, and throws GARLAND the bottle.*

JIM   *Psych!* I'm full'a shit. Hey? Hey?

> *GARLAND drinks.*

GARLAND   You *are* full'a shit.

JIM   I *am*. I am *full* of shit. And *he* is too if he wants anyone to believe that he just kinda *shoved* his dad and that's all, I don't believe that, you'd have to be stupid to believe that. But you know who is the *most* full of shit? You. You with your, I don't know what, about being ready to leave the program — *you're* ready, and *he's* ready, and Christ I don't know who else, but *I'm* not! *You're fucking him and he's underage! Aren't you?*

> *No answer.*

Aren't you?!

> *No answer.*

So, who's fulla shit?

GARLAND   It's consensual.

JIM   What's the difference?

GARLAND   He says it's okay, that's the difference.

JIM   He's under age. He can't give consent, asshole.

GARLAND   He knows what he's doing.

JIM   Bullshit!

GARLAND   Tell him.

JIM   Look at him! He doesn't know, okay! He'll do whatever for you. You're his fucking Hero— you're-taking-him-to-Vancouver-you're-going-to take-care-of-him. *You're* just doing what you've always done, getting what *you* want—

GARLAND You don't know what the fuck you're talking about!

JIM   —and you don't give a *shit* about him!

GARLAND He knows what he's doing*!*

JIM   He offed his old man and he's not even sure that's such a bad thing so don't tell me he knows what the fuck he's doing!

     Slight pause.

    And he's the guy *you* picked to go to Vancouver with. But hey, if that's your thing. *Young boys.* Fine. At least I'm honest, when I get out to the coast, I'm telling you right now I'm not going to say no to *anything* I want, *anywhere* I want, the park or whereever.

     Slight pause.

    So, we know where we're at. Right?

GARLAND Sure.

STUART   You going to tell?

JIM   Why would I want to tell?

     He sniffs more thinner.

    Let's just get the hell out of here. I can't stand fags.

     JIM stretches.

JIM   Get the hell outta here, and then we can get
             the hell outta each other's way. Fair
             enough?

GARLAND   It's okay with me.

STUART   Yea.

JIM   Okay.

             *With one outstretched arm, JIM grabs the vice
             that is resting on the work table, and bringing
             it up over his head sends it crashing down
             onto GARLAND's right leg, breaking it.
             GARLAND screams. JIM spins around and
             kicks GARLAND full in the face.*

JIM   The *fuck* I'm going to take your shit! I been
             taking shit *all* my life. *No more!*

             *He stalks over and takes the music box out of
             GARLAND's pocket.*

JIM   Gimme that! This is *my* gig! Take my
             stepdad's *shit*, and my mom's *shit*, stepsister's
             shit, everything taken from me all my life, I
             fucken do pay *back*—

             He delivers another kick to GARLAND.

JIM   — and give my stepsister a little taste of the
             crap I've had to swallow alla my life and *I
             get put away for it??* Get stuck in a group, while
             she sits at home in my house with my mother,
             my life — "The Victim" — and now you think
             I'm going take your shit? I trusted you!

             *JIM picks up a box of bottles and smashes
             them on GARLAND.*

JIM   *I trusted you!*

             He turns and advances on STUART.

JIM   And *you*! Everything was okay before you
                    came into it, everything was all right and
                    then *you* got involved. *We were going to
                    Vancouver! I had the remote! Well fuck you!*

                    *JIM grabs STUART and begins to throw him
                    around.*

STUART   Cut it out!

JIM   Shut your fuckin' mouth! I'll do what I want.

GARLAND   Leave him—

                    *STUART tries to fight back. JIM overpowers
                    him, punches him several times, then turns
                    him around and grinds his pelvis against
                    STUART'S rear.*

JIM   This the kind'a thing you do to him nights?
                    You and him? Is it?

                    *JIM throws STUART to the floor. He hovers
                    over STUART and unzips his fly.*

GARLAND   Jim!

                    GARLAND flings a box at JIM.

JIM   Leave me the fuck alone ya wus!

                    *JIM kicks GARLAND again. Then picks up
                    his head by the hair and slams it to the floor.
                    STUART tosses some paint thinner on JIM
                    and dashes to the work table. JIM turns and
                    chases STUART. STUART grabs the lighter,
                    flicks it and tosses it at JIM. JIM erupts in
                    flames. He screams, waves his arms around,
                    and throws himself to the floor.*

JIM   Help! Help! Help! Help!

GARLAND   Toss me the towel! Toss me the towel!

> *STUART doesn't respond. He simply stares at JIM as he burns.*
>
> *GARLAND crawls over to where the towel is, picks it up, crawls to JIM. GARLAND then lunges with the towel and placing it over JIM, smothers the flames. He lies there on top of JIM a moment. There is a long moment of silence.*

GARLAND   Jim? Jim?

> *JIM doesn't answer.*

We've screwed this up pretty good.

> *GARLAND shifts and groans.*

Ah, my leg. He busted it for sure.

> *Pause.*

STUART   Is he dead?

GARLAND   No.

> *Pause.*

STUART   Maybe we should...

GARLAND   What?

> *Pause.*

STUART   Kill him.

> *Pause. GARLAND stares up at STUART for a very long moment.*

GARLAND   I... (*clearing his throat which has suddenly gone dry*) I don't think so.

> *STUART picks up another thinner container.*

GARLAND   I don't think that's such a good idea, Stuart.

STUART   I don't know.

GARLAND   I think that would be, a real bad idea. I mean, they'd catch you for that for sure. And then you could count on some pretty severe lock up.

> *STUART takes the cap off the thinner. Tosses the cap aside.*

Listen. We go back, we take our lumps, we plan, you know, for another day. We go back, *with him,* like he is. And you tell them what happened, and me too — I'd back you up — and it's like self defense, you know? Self defense? They don't put guys in jail for that.

STUART   Who's ever listened to me?

GARLAND   Me. Me, and *I'd back you up.* I'd back you up, Stuart.

STUART   He wakes up, he'll tell. He'll tell everybody everything. I'm not going to go to prison.

> *STUART steps closer to JIM.*

GARLAND   I don't think you will man, I mean, I don't think you'll have to—

> *STUART begins to pour the thinner over JIM's body.*

(*continued*) But you torch him now, *you torch him,* when you didn't have to and him just lying there and we're really, truly fucked forever. I mean, *I* wouldn't even be able to understand that, man, and I can understand what you did to your Dad and other people will too. I mean, you were younger then and look at what he was doing to you ... all your life, right? I can see that. And other people will too.

The thinner bottle now empty, STUART tosses it aside. He picks up the lighter.

GARLAND   (*continued*) But this. This. You gotta listen to me, Stuart, cause I'm on your side.

I mean, I don't know what you thought when Jim was saying all that shit about us, about me taking advantage or whatever, and maybe sometimes I'm not thinking things through, you know, from your side, cause, cause — it's hard, getting everything right, in your mind about everything, but this is straight, *straight*, thinking of you. No bullshit. They'll put us away big time, Stuart. Both of us. They will.

Slight pause. The lighter remains in STUART's hand.

Come on, man, come on. We didn't, you know, go AWOL and all this shit just to get put in the pen, right? It's enough for tonight, eh? Stuart? It's enough.

STUART   I guess that's the end of the movies for us? I was looking forward to that.

GARLAND   They're not going to stop making them because we don't get there tonight, man. They can wait. We can wait.

STUART puts the lighter back in his pocket.

It's not gonna happen tomorrow, but it can happen.

GARLAND blinks as he realizes he's coming close to passing out.

GARLAND   You gonna call someone, Stu? I'm a... I'm pretty messed up here, and Jim's gotta see someone.

STUART   Who should I call?

GARLAND   911.

STUART   And say what?

GARLAND   Get an ambulance. I'm just gonna shut my eyes for a minute, man.

>*STUART steps out of the garage and re-enters with a phone.*

STUART   An ambulance? Garland?

>*GARLAND doesn't answer. STUART dials the number.*

Hello? We've had an accident. We need an ambulance.

(*listening*) Where am I? I don't know. Garland, what's the address here? Garland? (*back into the phone*) I don't know. I don't know the neighborhood. We're... We're in a garage.

>*Fade to black.*

>*The End.*